PAT'S MAP

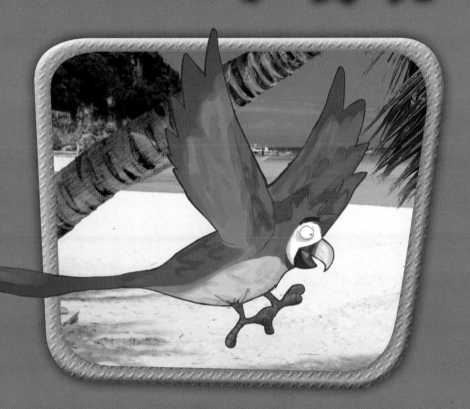

Written by Monica Hughes

Illustrated by Michael Emmerson

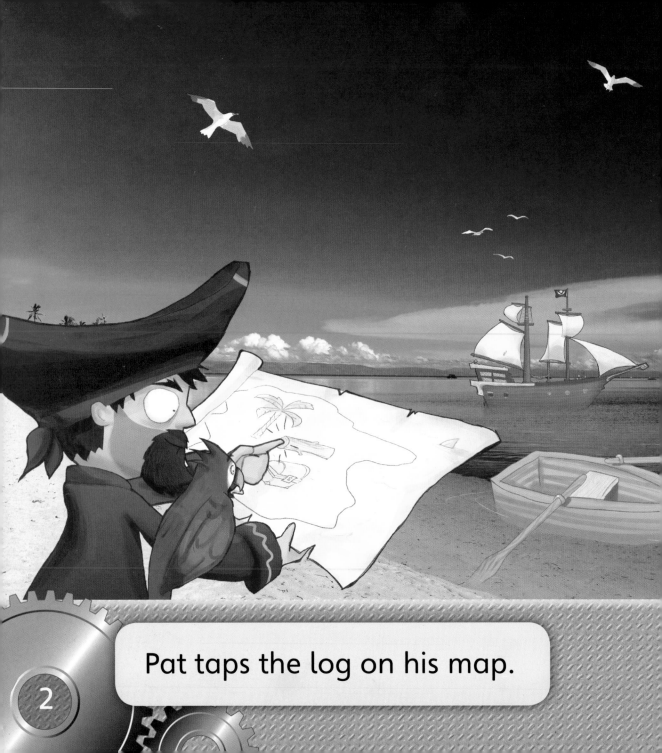

Pat taps the log on his map.

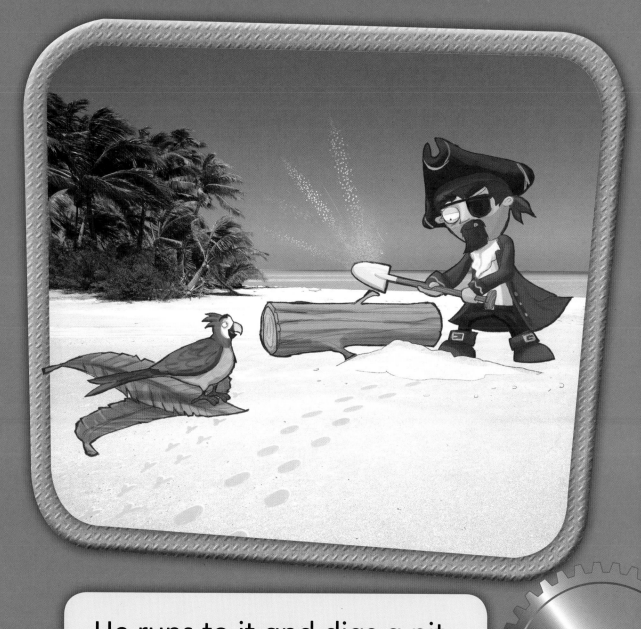

He runs to it and digs a pit.

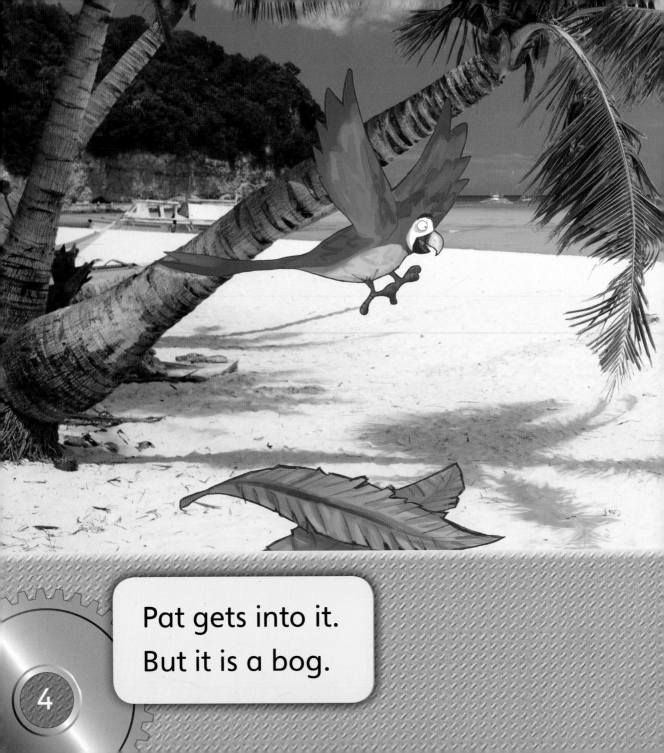

Pat gets into it.
But it is a bog.

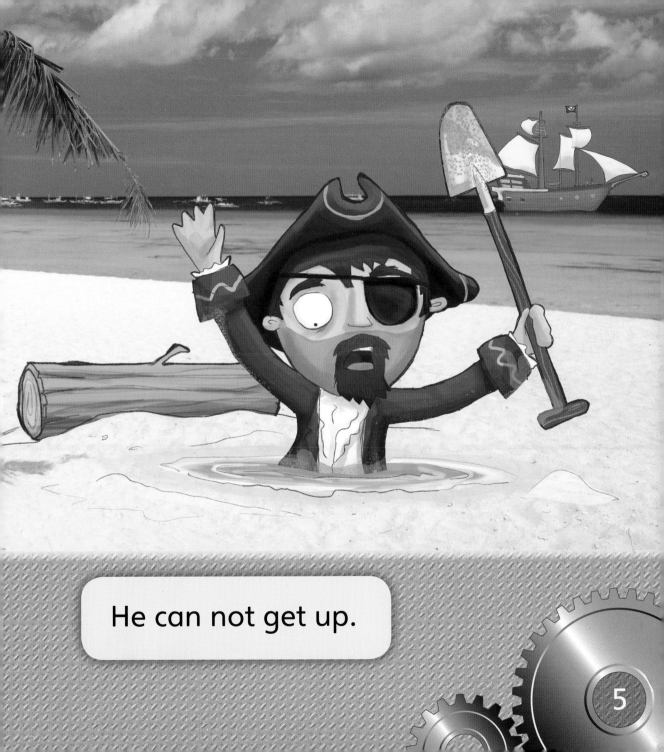

He can not get up.

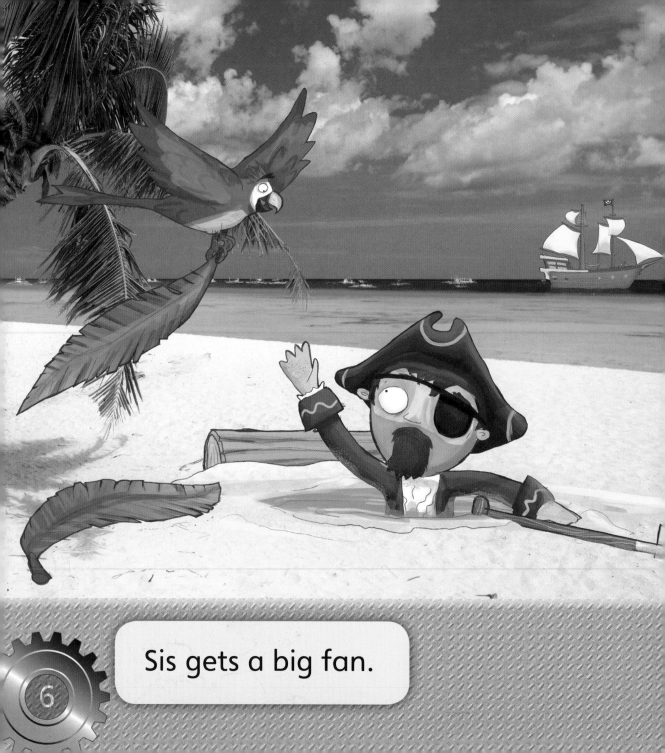

Sis gets a big fan.

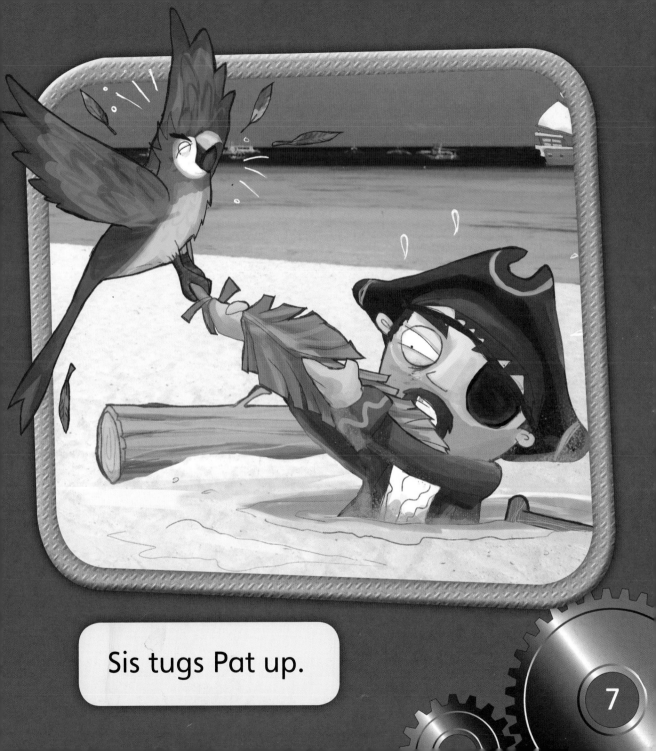

Sis tugs Pat up.

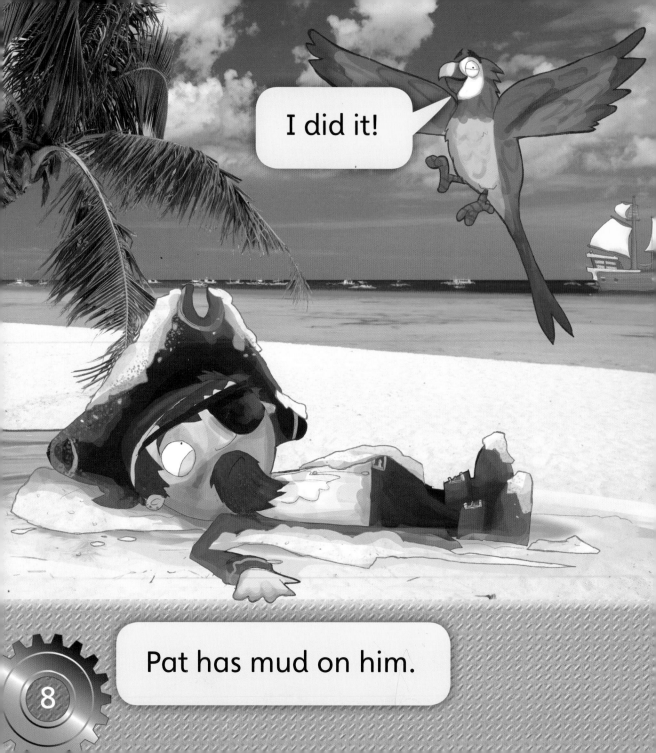

Pat has mud on him.